Bibliographical Series
of Supplements to ' British Book News '

★

GENERAL EDITOR
T. O. Beachcroft

Supplement to *British Book News*

TOBIAS
SMOLLETT

By LAURENCE BRANDER

PUBLISHED FOR

THE BRITISH COUNCIL
and the NATIONAL BOOK LEAGUE
by LONGMANS, GREEN & CO.
LONDON. NEW YORK. TORONTO

ice One Shilling and Sixpence

In this essay Laurence Brander writes not only of Smollett's famous contribution to the art of the novel, but also of his lesser-known work in building up the profession of literature during the eighteenth century. He describes the character and personality of the industrious, kindly, and yet irascible man who left Scotland and, after a few years in the Navy, settled down to a life of editing and literary production in London, of which his great novels were only a part.

Laurence Brander is himself a Scot who has travelled widely and devoted his life to letters. He was born in 1903 and educated in Edinburgh. He lectured in English literature in Lucknow University, and during his twelve years in India he published a number of books with the Indian Branch of the Oxford University Press, including a Prosody and Rhetoric.

In 1939 he returned to England and went to Oxford University, where he worked on Thomas Hood until the war broke in. He joined the staff of the British Broadcasting Corporation, was their first representative in Delhi and afterwards was associated with the late George Orwell in the publication of literary broadcasts to India. After the war he joined the Oxford University Press, and three years later became Director of Publications in the British Council. His latest book is a selection of Robert Burns in the World's Classics.

TOBIAS SMOLLETT
*from a painting about 1770 by an unknown Italian
artist, in the National Portrait Gallery*

TOBIAS SMOLLETT

By LAURENCE BRANDER

PUBLISHED FOR
THE BRITISH COUNCIL
and the NATIONAL BOOK LEAGUE
BY LONGMANS, GREEN & CO., LONDON, NEW YORK, TORONTO

LONGMANS, GREEN & CO. LTD.
6 & 7 Clifford Street, London, W.1
Also at Melbourne and Cape Town

LONGMANS, GREEN & CO. INC.
55 Fifth Avenue, New York, 3

LONGMANS, GREEN & CO.
215 Victoria Street, Toronto, 1

ORIENT LONGMANS LTD.
Bombay, Calcutta, Madras

First Published in 1951

Printed in Great Britain by Benham and Company Limited
Colchester

TOBIAS SMOLLETT

I

THE portrait of Smollett in the National Portrait Gallery suggests a man of intelligence, energy, and determination. The long self-portrait in his *Travels through France and Italy* suggests the same virtues, along with a sharp sort of humour not far removed from the spleen. The two went together in eighteenth century authorship with very enjoyable results.

In his last novel, *Humphry Clinker*, Smollett introduces a picture of his earlier life in Chelsea, and in this picture there is a self-portrait:

> By all accounts, Smollett is not without weakness and caprice, but he is certainly good humoured and civilized : nor do I find that there is anything overbearing, cruel or implacable in his disposition.

Autobiography is a dangerous weakness; everything that is put in or left out can be used against the writer. Weakness and caprice are the common human lot and only a strong man will make a claim against them. Good humour and being civilized are virtues which every eighteenth-century man would wish to claim; but why should Smollett, a writer who balanced his words, claim that he was not over-bearing, cruel, or implacable unless the charge had been made against him with some force?

The charges which can be brought against him as author of *Roderick Random* and *Peregrine Pickle* are those which will be brought to-day against the author of picaresque novels, and will include cruelty. The other epithets could have been earned by his journalism when he was a dominating figure in literary London from 1750 to 1762. He was possibly the outstanding figure in literary London between the death of Pope and the great reign of Johnson.

In the picture already referred to Smollett says:

> I saw none of the usual signs of authorship, either in the house or in the landlord, who is one of those few writers of the age

that stand upon their own foundation, without patronage and above dependence.

But for Johnson's famous letter to Lord Chesterfield (' Is not a Patron, my Lord, one who looks with unconcern on a man struggling for life in the water, and, when he has reached ground, encumbers him with help? ') this might have become the common quotation in literary histories to mark a change over from patronage to another economic system of authorship.

Smollett ran a literary factory in Chelsea while Johnson was running one in Pump Court, off the Strand, for his dictionary. Both claimed independence from patronage: neither stressed their dependence upon other writers who were capable of hard work and incapable of dealing to advantage with the publishers. Independence is a claim that does not bear sifting. Both were good business men, working with energy and enterprise for the general good of authorship.

Smollett was an innovator in literary kinds and methods. He was the first to publish a long historical work in weekly parts at a popular price; he was the first to publish a full-length novel as a serial in a weekly journal. He raised critical standards by editing for seven years an independent journal in the days when most critical reviews were subsidized advertisement sheets for the publishers.

Smollett is known to-day as the author of three novels and a book of travels, but his life story is one of immense literary activity and energy. Placed against that forgotten work, these four books seem almost by-products; which is the way great imaginative books are sometimes written. Smollett was an entrepreneur in literature, a doctor by profession, who burst upon literary society with a successful novel at the age of twenty-seven, repeated his success three years later, and gave up his first profession to devote his extraordinary energy to literature. He wanted to organize it, to found an Academy, to improve the conditions of authorship and to improve criticism so that writing would improve and fulfil its function in society.

He failed. The memory of his efforts has almost disappeared and all the volume of writing, in journalism, criticism, compilation, and history which he did himself and inspired in others has been forgotten.

He was a Scotsman, born of good family in Dumbartonshire in 1721. He studied medicine in Glasgow and very soon, in the familiar Scots way, he went to London. He joined the Navy as a surgeon, and went on the Carthegena Expedition in 1741. This was part of the maritime war with Spain begun in 1739 about South American trade. The Navy had not been on active service for a long time and the Expedition was badly organized and ended in disaster. Smollett wrote a pamphlet on the subject, one of his first attacks on muddle-headed stupidity. His experiences gave him copy for his novels, so that it might almost be said that the best things that came out of the Expedition were the sailors in *Roderick Random* and *Peregrine Pickle* and the satirical treatment of it in *Roderick Random*.

Smollett found a wife in Jamaica and settled in London in 1744 to practise medicine from a house in Downing Street. He was living near by in Mayfair in 1746 when the news of the battle of Culloden broke on London and the citizens went Mafeking-mad with relief after being hysterical with fear of invasion by the Scots and their Stuart claimant to the throne. Two or three years later, he settled in Chelsea, where he worked as a writer until his health broke in 1762. Chelsea was then a small town and the road to the City of Westminster was sometimes the hunting ground of footpads and highwaymen. The soft air of Chelsea seems to have been as congenial to authorship then as it is now.

From 1763 to 1765 Smollett lived in France and Italy, spending most of the time at Nice. He returned to England and spent much of his time travelling; and when he was not travelling he lived in Bath, at that time a focus for English society. In 1768 he returned to northern Italy, for so many years an author's annexe for England, and settled down in a house near Leghorn, where he died in 1771. He was buried in the English cemetery there, an old, neglected place now; how different from the English cemetery in Lisbon, bright with flowers, where Fielding lies.

II

The forgotten mass of his work may be considered first, as it is relevant to the study of the four books which are read to-day.

Smollett seems to have begun his career as a journalist by working on the *Monthly Review* for Ralph Griffiths, the bookseller in St. Paul's Churchyard. It was after some experience of this kind of work that he wrote:

> The miserable author must perform his daily task, in spite of cramp, colick, vapours, or vertigo ; in spite of head-ach, heart-ach, and *Minerva's* frowns ; other wise he will lose his character and livelihood, like a taylor who disappoints his customers in a birth-day suit.

In 1755 he broke away and projected a new journal which he called the *Criticial Review*. From 1756 until his breakdown in 1762 he controlled its policy and no doubt used his factory for producing copy.

The proposals for this *Review*, which he called *Proposals for publishing Monthly, The Progress or Annals of Literature and the Liberal Arts*, appeared in the last days of 1755. They indicate the position which this young man hoped to fill in the London literary world of the mid-eighteenth century.

> This Work will not be patched up by obscure Hackney Writers, accidentally enlisted in the Service of an undistinguishing Bookseller, [so much for Master Ralph Griffiths and his ilk] but executed by a Set of Gentlemen whose Characters and Capacities have been universally approved and acknowledged by the Public : Gentlemen, who have long observed with Indignation the Productions of Genius and Dullness ;

Wit and Impertinence ; Learning and Ignorance, confounded in the Chaos of Publication ; applauded without Taste and condemned without Distinction ; and who have seen the noble Art of Criticism reduced to a contemptible Manufacture subservient to the most sordid Views of Avarice and Interest, and carried on by wretched Hirelings, without Talent, Candour, Spirit or Circumspection.[1]

The tone of these *Proposals* indicates the fervour of Smollett's campaigning in early maturity for a better literary London. His scheme for an Academy of Letters never got nearer to realization than in these Proposals, and in the conduct of the *Critical Review*.

His immense energies were absorbed at the same time in his *Complete History of England, Deduced from the Descent of Julius Caesar to the Treaty of Aix La Chapelle, 1748. Containing the Transactions of One Thousand Eight Hundred and Three Years.* He worked on it from 1755 to 1757 and it was published in four handsome quarto volumes in 1757 and 1758. His contract to James Rivington and James Fletcher seems to have been for the first three quartos which were published together in April 1757, bringing the history up to the end of the reign of William and Mary. The fourth volume appeared eight months later. The idea appears to have come from the booksellers who got it from Hume's *History*, which began publication in 1754 and was completed in 1761. Hume published in Edinburgh and the London booksellers probably hired Smollett so that they could exploit the idea for London sales. It was certainly not a Tory answer to Hume's sceptical and Whig approach, for Smollett began with Whig leanings and only later on, as he worked, did he discover a Tory outlook.

He revised the whole thing in 1758 for publication in weekly parts at sixpence, showing good publishing sense in doing so and being the first writer in London who published a history in a popular format. He told Dr. Moore that orders rose to 10,000 and there is a story that his publishers

[1] *Public Advertiser*, 30 December 1755.

addressed an early part to every parish clerk in the country, enclosing half a crown and asking them to push sales by letting people see it.

In 1760 Smollett began publishing a *Continuation* to his *History*, planning forty sixpenny parts covering the twelve years from the end of 1748. This contemporary survey was admirably written with an urbanity very different from the scratching and biting attacks so common in his journalism. The *Continuation* made amends for all that, and he took the opportunity of the aloof approach of the historian to write of his contemporaries with detachment, good sense, and often with magnificent compliment. This *Continuation* was used during the next eighty years at the end of Hume's *History*, often with title pages which suggested that Smollett sat down in the first place to continue Hume.

The labour of the *History* undermined his health. He wrote it down in Chelsea, it is said in fourteen months, working with absurd concentration, refusing himself to callers, worried by debt and by duns and with it all laying himself open to the tuberculosis which then first attacked him and eventually killed him.

During this intensive historical writing he at least allowed himself the luxury of other kinds of writing, for in 1756 he wrote *The Reprisal*, a brief play for performance after the main piece which was produced by Garrick in 1757 at the Theatre Royal in Drury Lane. This was generous of Garrick and when Smollett revised *Peregrine Pickle* in 1758 the satire on Garrick's acting was removed.

In the beginning of 1760 he launched *The British Magazine*, which ran till 1767. Much work for it had been prepared prudently before the journal was launched, and it is distinguished by carrying some of the finest essays of Oliver Goldsmith. It was here that *Sir Launcelot Greaves* appeared in serial form.

Meanwhile, also, he continued to be the life and soul of the *Critical Review*. On one occasion he cast doubts upon the courage of an Admiral, who dealt with him in peremptory sailor fashion and in November 1760 Smollett disappeared for eleven weeks into the Marshalsea prison. Prison conditions were made easy for him and apparently his writing went on without interruption.

He was engaged furthermore all this time in translation work and in the oversight of the immense compilations his literary factory produced.

Finally and unfortunately he was persuaded to edit the *Briton*, a political weekly which appeared from May 1762 to February 1763 in defence of Bute's ministry. Here he walked into real trouble, for his chief opponent was his old friend John Wilkes, who was so much the master of Smollett at this kind of work that he scored off him with the greatest of ease. The *Briton* formed a focus for attacks on the Scots, at that time peculiarly unpopular in London, and Wilkes at the head of the local brigade of political journalists smiled and smote in the *North Briton*. This was bad enough for anyone as sensitive as Smollett. What was worse was the corroding effect of an excursion into politics on an eager and spirited worker for the betterment of society. It ended as it was bound to end, in bitter disillusionment.

By the summer of 1762 Smollett was seriously ill and eventually in the summer of 1763 he cut himself away from all his burdens and went to France and Italy. This record of his writing up to his illness marks his extraordinary energy. He always worked well and sometimes with genius. All the time he was urged on by the belief that if only man would think and organize, society would progress to happiness. Especially, he was haunted by a belief that the world of letters would exert its proper influence if it were organized.

All this journalism died with him. It was popular at the time, apart from the political stuff, but it has never been read since and his great efforts for improving literature and the arts, whether by academies or by improving periodical criticism, have left no apparent result.   None of it, except the *History* and its *Continuation*, has ever been reprinted.

The Adventures of an Atom (1769) must have been written during his last stay in Britain, some time after the period of his great activity just described.   It is a vindictive satire of current affairs and public characters from 1754 to the date of publication and it is Smollett's last fling at the politicians before he left them for ever.   It could hardly be further away from the urbanity of his *Continuation*.   The fiction under which the satire is maintained is that an atom moves from Japan to the brain of one Nathaniel Peacock, and dictates what he must write of its ' Japonese ' adventures. Any doubts about the true subject matter are dispelled in an early paragraph, which is an unmistakable portrait of the English people :

> The Japonese value themselves much upon their constitution, and are very clamorous about the words liberty and property ; yet, in fact, the only liberty they enjoy is to get drunk when they please, to revile the government, and quarrel with one another. With respect to their property, they are the tamest animals in the world ; and, if properly managed, undergo, without wincing, such impositions as no other nation in the world would bear.

Soon there follows the exceptionally disgusting descriptions which make all devout critics ignore the book or deny that Smollett wrote it.   Yet immediately afterwards the prose pictures of ministers are so good that they recall Dryden's verse pictures.   Pages of explosive virulence follow, directed against military and naval commanders, every statesman in the country and especially Chatham.   The common people, the political mob, are almost the most loathly of all.   Indeed the text of the book might be Swift's ' I cannot but conclude the Bulk of your Natives, to be the most pernicious Race of little odious Vermin that Nature ever suffered to crawl upon the Surface of the Earth '.

The Swiftian rancorous spleen is in Smollett's performance, but nothing of Swift's peculiar greatness, nothing of the ease, almost the magnanimity, of Swift's condemnation of the human race. Smollett has a smaller man's concentrated virulence and eventually a certain weariness with the whole performance overtakes the reader. Perhaps Smollett did not write it. He never admitted authorship : and friendly critics have always either denied his authorship or left the question open. Yet, so many of these characters are so well done, and so many of the sentences are quotable and memorable ; and the main unpleasant theme, the sycophancy of public life, is so much Smollett's lifelong special hate that it is difficult to suggest he had nothing to do with it. If Smollett did not write it, what other perverted genius did?

III

We come now to the three novels and the book of travels which are generally read to-day. Smollett was third of the four writers who set the English novel on its way. *Roderick Random* was published in 1748, in the same year as Richardson's *Clarissa*, and within the decade which saw the great beginnings. *Pamela* (1740) begat Fielding's *Joseph Andrews* (1742) and *Tom Jones* followed in 1749. In 1751 came *Peregrine Pickle*, with its obvious inspiration to Sterne's *Tristram Shandy* (1760–7). *Humphry Clinker* (1771) completed the series which set the novel on its way.

According to the picaresque convention, Smollett claims a satirical and reforming intention in the preface to *Roderick Random* :

> Of all kinds of satire, there is none so entertaining and universally improving, as that which is introduced, as it were, occasionally.

The reader is a sensible and sober citizen, who must have some excuse for enjoying a book in which the morals are those of a thieves' kitchen. The same convention is used in *Gil Blas*, which Smollett translated and published in 1749.

It had been used, with much greater comic skill, by Fielding in the opening of *Jonathan Wild* (1743). Smollett blurs his comedy by breaking seriously into satire, especially in his descriptions of life in the Navy. Indeed, he seems to have chosen picaresque, with the familiar gallery of odd characters, usually criminal types, strung together in a series of episodes, because he had a grudge against society. He had tried verse as a vehicle for his satire, and had failed ; he would now try prose.

Roderick Random is the orphaned, unwanted grandson of a severe old Scots magistrate, exposed by his grandfather's known neglect to the malice of the community. His principal enemies are the schoolmaster and the young heir. It is not long before a *deus ex machina* appears in the form of a sailor uncle, and for the first time a British tar appears in the English novel :

> He was a strongly built man, somewhat bandy-legged, with a neck like that of a bull, and a face which (you might easily perceive) had withstood the most obstinate assaults of the weather. His dress consisted of a soldier's coat, altered for him by the ship's tailor, a striped flannel jacket, a pair of red breeches japanned with pitch, clean grey worsted stockings, large silver buckles that covered three-fourths of his shoes, a silver laced hat whose crown overlooked the brim about an inch and a half, a black bob wig in buckle, a check shirt, a silk hankerchief, a hanger with a brass handle girded on his thigh by a tarnished laced belt, and a good oak plant under his arm.

What a subject for the publisher of illustrated editions— ' red breeches japanned with pitch ' ! This excellent officer proceeds at once to discomfit the heir, flog the schoolmaster and interview grandfather. His speech is as good as his costume and for the first time we hear the salt spray accents in English fiction :

> Your servant, your servant. What cheer, father? What cheer? I suppose you don't know me ; mayhap you don't. My name is Tom Bowling, and this here boy : you look as if you did not know him neither ; 'tis like you mayn't. He's new rigg'd i' faith ; his cloth don't shake in the wind so much

as it wont to do. 'Tis my nephew, d'ye see, Roderick Random, your own flesh and blood, old gentleman. ' Don't lay astern you dog ! ' pulling me forward.

' The Navy's here ' once again and for a while all goes well with Roderick Random. But the sailor returns to sea, leaving the youngster settled with a Mr. Potion, the apothecary in a neighbouring town, who turns him away when misfortune overtakes Tom Bowling. Mr. Crab, the surgeon, takes him in, because it will harm Potion, his rival. His school friends and relations melt away, and incident after incident reflects the cynicism of the young novelist.

His virtues as a writer are already apparent in these early chapters. He has the golden pen, the style which wraps one round. Characters and incidents follow one another in teeming plenty and only a strong stomach is required to carry the reader forward, ready to follow Roderick Random anywhere. And indeed, there is some exertion in travelling, or there would be but for the easy vehicle of this fine eighteenth-century prose. Character after character appears, sketched with the clear crudeness of an old woodcut, or designed as it were for the caricaturists like Rowlandson who were to spring from this English society as naturally as Smollett himself. Crab, the surgeon, is a good example of this prodigality for here he is, and he lasts only for a part of a chapter:

> This member of the faculty was aged fifty, about five feet high, and ten round the belly ; his face was capacious as a full moon, and much of the complexion of a mulberry ; his nose resembled a powder-horn, was swelled to an enormous size, and studded all over with carbuncles ; and his little grey eyes reflected the rays in such an oblique manner, that while he looked a person full in the face, one would have imagined he was admiring the buckle of his shoe.

Excellent average eighteenth century, matched later only by Dickens, who profited by study of Smollett.

There is no resisting these characters and these incidents unless we are built so that they are both too harsh and too gross for us. We may find it difficult to realize, partly because of this harshness, partly because of the remoteness of eighteenth-century society, that for Smollett and his reader this was a picture of contemporary life in which many known characters were recognizable.

The hero eventually joins the Navy as a doctor, which gives Smollett his opportunity to describe with minuteness and trenchancy the inefficient methods of recruitment at that time. Eventually he puts to sea, and the first of the long series of stories of the Silent Service begins.

It is at once apparent that there was much besides perfec-tion to keep the Navy silent in those days, for Smollett is concerned to describe the evil conditions on ships. (' A man had better go to prison than go to sea ', said Dr. Johnson) and to expose the incompetent management of the Carthe-gina Expedition. This celebration of the character of the Navy and its sailors is the best part of the book. The ocean and the winds of the world form the background to many English stories of the little societies of men on ships ; and the special atmosphere of these seafaring societies against their elemental background is caught in *Roderick Random* for the first time. While Smollett was writing, the British Empire was in the making and the two great influences of vast land and sea spaces, so different from island atmos-phere, were beginning their work on the English character.

The great ocean influence is nowhere consciously stated by Smollett as it is by Conrad,[1] but it is inherent in his subject.

The indignation of the young doctor at conditions at sea finds trenchant expression :

> I assisted Thomson in making up his prescriptions : but when I followed him with the medicines into the sick berth or hospital, and observed the situation of the patients, I was much less surprised that people should die on board, than that any sick person should recover. Here I saw about fifty miserable distempered wretches, suspended in rows so huddled upon one

[1] See Oliver Warner's *Joseph Conrad* in this series.

another that not more than fourteen inches space was allotted
for each with his bed and bedding ; and deprived of the light
of the day as well as of fresh air ; breathed nothing but a
noisome atmosphere of the morbid steams exhaling from their
own excrements and diseased bodies, devoured with vermin
that hatched in the filth that surrounded them, and destitute
of every convenience necessary for people in that helpless
condition

Smollett's descriptive comments on the Carthegina Expedition are of a kind to which we have grown accustomed
after two world wars. Smollett's treatment is classical,
for no expedition could exceed the Cartheginan in the
stupidity of its conduct and no writer could surpass the
happy gusto of this young genius.

Chapter 33 is a *locus classicus* for all war commentators.
Smollett makes short shift with the tactics of the commanders, writing for example of a particularly atrocious tactical
blunder :

> This piece of conduct afforded matter of speculation to all
> the wits either in the Army or Navy, who were at last fain to
> acknowledge it a stroke of policy above their comprehension.

He deals with the medical and quarter-master's arrange-
ments with equal delight. Yet it is not for these things that
Roderick Random is celebrated as the first of our naval
novels, but for the descriptions of sailors, of storms at sea,
and of the never-failing wonder at what common men can
endure against the elements and their leaders.

Eventually the hero returns to England and lands not in
any normal way, for this is a picaresque novel, but by ship-
wreck and in fighting with his shipmates on the shore.

The normal adventures of a picaresque hero then follow.
He becomes manservant in a local family and falls in love
with the young lady of the house, the fair Narcissa. He
goes abroad and serves as a common soldier in the French
Army, which gives an opportunity for discussing the battle

of Dettingen.[1]   His old friend Strap reappears to rescue
him.   These sudden reappearances of favourite characters
to prove the truth of the adapted saying, ' cast your bread
upon the waters and it will come back buttered after many
days ' is a piece of machinery frequently used.   Thomson,
who threw himself overboard in despair, survived to feed
and outfit the hero and set him on his way in Jamaica.   In
the end his father comes to life again and restores the family
fortunes so that the hero, now an undoubted gentleman,
rent-roll and all, can marry Narcissa.   It is all engagingly
simple, and supplies the only continuity the plot boasts.

The picaresque atmosphere is oppressive, principally
because of the moral concepts the hero follows.   He must
never work honestly for his living.   He may fight duels,
gamble, try to marry for money and accept whatever he
needs from his equals and agents.   He may not be cowardly
or mean, rather he must be foolishly brave and foolishly
generous.   His enemies may outwit him, but in the end
picaresque justice demands that the hero or his good fortune
overcomes them.   It is never suggested that he is an enemy
of society or that society has a case against him.   The quarrels
are all with individuals and there is no hint that behind it
all there may be a social structure which is damaged by his
conduct.   The sense of social structure only comes at the
end, for he must be admitted again to honourable place (that
is, position and money) so that he may marry and live
happily ever afterwards.

The next novel, *Peregrine Pickle*, is equally offensive to us
in these ways.   It is rescued from being utterly sordid by
the great character, Commodore Hawser Trunnion and
his shipmates, retired from the sea and settled on land as
part of English village society.   The hero rises out of English
village society, which is to say average English society in

[1] Though nothing he has to say of it matches this note to his satire,
Advice (1746) : ' This line relates to the behaviour of a General on a
certain occasion : who discovered an extreme passion for the cool shade
during the heat of the day : the Hanoverian General, in the battle of
Dettingen.'

those days. This brings the novel nearer to Fielding, who had an unfailing sense of social structure. Smollett usually preferred the shifting scene of London, where many societies have their own laws and customs.

Trunnion is so much more real than any character in the first novel that it may be described as a rapid development since *Peregrine Pickle* was first published in 1751, only three years later. It was heavily revised by Smollett and re-published in 1758, about fifty pages shorter, the slanderous sketches of contemporaries being removed. It is invariably the revised edition which is reprinted to-day.

Commodore Trunnion was as lost ashore as a whale. He garrisoned himself with old shipmates against all the perils of the land, and chief amongst these were women and lawyers. When everyone, including the garrison, leagued against him to marry him, he was lost and in a brief passage of high comedy, which is one of the most delicious things in the eighteenth-century novel, he makes his proposals of matrimony.

On the wedding day the groom set out on horseback ' at the head of all his male attendants, whom he had rigged with the white shirts and black caps formerly belonging to his barge's crew '. Yet he did not arrive in time, indeed the bridal party

> waited a whole half hour for the commodore, at whose slow-ness they began to be under some apprehension, and accordingly dismissed a servant to quicken his pace. The valet, having rode something more than a mile, espied the whole troop disposed in a long file, crossing the road obliquely, and headed by the bridegroom and his friend Hatchway, who, finding himself hindered by a hedge from proceeding farther in the same direction, fired a pistol, and stood over to the other side, making an obtuse angle with the line of his former course ; and the rest of the squadron followed his example, keeping always in the rear of each other like a flight of wild geese.
>
> Surprised at this strange method of journeying, the messenger came up, and told the commodore that his lady and her company

expected him in the church, where they had tarried a considerable time, and were beginning to be very uneasy at his delay ; and therefore desired he would proceed with more expedition. To this message Mr. Trunnion replied, ' Hark ye, brother, don't you see we make all possible speed? Go back, and tell those who sent you, that the wind has shifted since we weighed anchor, and that we are obliged to make very short trips in tacking, by reason of the narrowness of the channel ; and that, as we lie within six points of the wind, they must make some allowance for variation and leeway'. ' Lord, sir ! ' said the valet, ' what occasion have you to go zig-zag in that manner? Do but clap spurs to your horses, and ride straight forward, and I'll engage you shall be at the church porch in less than a quarter of an hour.' 'What ! right in the wind's eye,' answered the commander ; ' ahey ! brother, where did you learn your navigation? Hawser Trunnion is not to be taught at this time of day how to lie his course, or keep his own reckoning. And as for you, brother, you best know the trim of your own frigate.'

Apart from the Trunnion group, which was so finely conceived that it inspired Sterne's Uncle Toby and his friends in *Tristram Shandy*, the old coarseness and sordid atmosphere remain and these qualities haunted Smollett in his next two novels and only left him in his great final masterpiece. There was some quirk in his nature which drove him, as through his early books it drove George Orwell later, to expend his genius on description of filth. And there is no doubt that Smollett's medical training gave added force to this idiosyncracy.

Peregrine Pickle is essentially similar in kind to *Roderick Random*, but Commodore Trunnion with his counterpart Lieutenant Hatchway and his retinue of sailors make it the greater book. This is not only by their own value as characters but because they acquire their full value by contrast with Peregrine's household and society in the village inn, which introduce, if only for a short space in the book's great length, good normal contemporary eighteenth-century English country life. The poorest part of the book is the long interruption ' The Memoirs of a Lady of Quality '

which Smollett's publishing sense of good-selling exclusive
scandal made him include and certainly gave the book
notoriety when it was published, but remains now a very
deadly dull appendage.

His next novel, *Ferdinand Count Fathom* (1753) is plain
picaresque and shows how poor the kind can be when no
sailors or other bright characters come to relieve the tedium
of repeated similar incident.   *Sir Launcelot Greaves* (1760–1)
was a contemporary English *Dox Quixote* and the reader
may get some amusement from it if he is good enough to
ignore the fact that the hero would have been arrested after
the first adventure.

Two books, the best Smollett wrote, and heartily to be
commended to any reader, remain for consideration.   In
the *Travels through France and Italy* Smollett is an early
example of the personal travel writer, conforming to Mr.
Norman Douglas's specification that it is the mind of the
traveller that matters.   Some of his comments are famous ;
his suggestion that a Corniche road would pay dividends ;
his forecast of trouble for France as soon as there was a
weak monarch ; his remark on the natural use of the
Borghese as a gallery ; his recommendation that the Roman
Campania be drained and cultivated—adopted as it were
only yesterday ; the commonplace that the entry to London
from the south is a disgrace to any metropolis—which is
being worked on to-day but largely remains for a better
to-morrow.

This is probably the first English book of travel which is
interesting because it reflects the state of a man's mind ;
the first of a kind in which English writers have displayed
a special aptitude.   The state of Smollett's mind when he
set out is described by himself :

> Traduced by malice, persecuted by faction, abandoned by
> false patrons, and overwhelmed by the sense of a domestic
> calamity, which it was not in the power of fortune to repair.

Echoes there of the *Briton*, of his service to Lord Bute,
who discarded him ; of Wilkes, who laid about him ; and

of the loss of his fifteen-year-old daughter, from which he
and his wife never recovered. The *Travels* were written
as he went along in the form of letters addressed to the circle
of Scots doctors in London who were his close friends,
and we may pleasantly presume that these physicians had a
talk amongst themselves before he left. They knew how ill
Smollett was, and they knew that part of the cure would
be for him to escape from the exertions of daily writing ;
but they also knew that it would be unwise for him to stop
suddenly and altogether ; so they proposed the letters or
encouraged him when he made the suggestion, explaining
how useful a record of inns, prices, and methods of transport
would be to them if they wished to make the Tour themselves. So Smollett tells them exactly what he thought of
the inns between London and Dover, and all the inn-
keepers he suffered from in France and Italy. He offered
detailed and apparently sound advice on transport, and he
told them of the cost of living everywhere.

He discussed water supplies and food as one doctor to
others. More personally he describes the state of his health,
and in one letter (the only one which opens ' Dear Doctor ')
he describes his exchange of letters with a French specialist
on tuberculosis.

Two letters, the seventh and fifteenth, are addressed to
the wife of one of the doctors (was it Mrs. Moore?). The
first was the famous attack on the French and the second
was an attack on duelling, a subject chosen carefully for his
correspondent after her reproof about his harsh judgement
of the French, to whom he makes amends in the opening of
the later letter.

In the other thirty-nine letters one of the finest living
English journalists addresses an audience fit and few over
a period of two years. The first is dated Boulogne, June
1763, and he is delighted to have left England. In the last,
Boulogne, June 1765, he is greatly recovered in body and
spirit and records his pleasure at seeing again ' the white
cliffs of Dover '.

He is an honest travel critic. ' I assure you, upon my word and honour, I have described nothing but what actually fell under my own observation.' Moreover, he says what he thought, and not what he should have thought. He was disappointed in Paris and Rome, and what honest traveller is not at first disappointed in places he has read about all his life and then first sees?

The less-known places are different. The shock of surprise can be pure pleasure, as in Smollett's first sight of the Maison Carrée at Nîmes :

> The proportions of the building are so happily united, as to give it an air of majesty and grandeur, which the most indifferent spectator cannot behold without emotion. A man need not be a connoisseur in architecture, to enjoy these beauties. They are indeed so exquisite that you may return to them every day with a fresh appetite for seven years together. . . . Without all doubt it is ravishingly beautiful. The whole world cannot parallel it ; and I am astonished to see it standing entire, like the effects of enchantment, after such a succession of ages, every one more barbarous than another.

That was written in Montpellier in November 1763. By September Boulogne had become too cold and Smollett heard that Nice was an ideal wintering place. He reached it in December and stayed there until the autumn of the following year, when he went to Italy. The letters from Nice, as from Boulogne, are full of people and places and all the other things which would delight his correspondents. In Italy he spent most of his time in Florence and Rome and his letters are full of art criticism and a vast deal of Latin learning. His taste in painting was very different from ours, and he enjoyed sculpture more, lingering with an anatomist's pleasure over the sculpture in the Pincio. But he always had space for what was present and lively. The English lived then in and around the Piazza D'Espagna,[1] and he remarks :

> When you arrive at Rome, you receive cards from all your

[1] Where Keats and Severn had rooms sixty years later.

country-folks in that city : they expect to have the visit returned
next day : when they give orders not to be at home ; and
you never speak a word to one another in the sequel. This
is a refinement in hospitality and politeness, which the English
have invented by the strength of their own genius, without any
assistance either from France, Italy or Lapland.

All through the *Travels* Smollett is at his best in the quick
sketches of inns and inn-keepers, postilions, and travellers.
The worst of them, and so the best to read about, were
between Nice and Genoa. At Noli :

> We ascended by a dark, narrow, steep stair, into a kind of
> public room, with a long table and benches, so dirty and
> miserable, that it would disgrace the worst hedge ale-house in
> England. . . . At length the landlord arrived, and gave us
> to understand, that he could accommodate us with chambers.
> In that where I lay, there was just room enough for two beds,
> without curtains or bedstead, an old rotten table covered with
> dried figs, and a couple of crazy chairs. The walls had once
> been white-washed : but were now hung with cobwebs, and
> speckled with dirt of all sorts, and I believe the brick-floor had
> not been swept for half a century.

A night or two later :

> At the post-house in Lerici, the accommodation is intolerable.
> We were almost poisoned at supper. I found the place where
> I was to lie so close and confined. that I could not breathe in it,
> and lay all night in an outward room upon four chairs, with a
> leather portmanteau for my pillow.

What happened on these occasions to poor Mrs. Smollett
we are never told. No fellow traveller could be more dim.
Only once, when Smollett flew into a rage at an inn outside
Florence and insisted on defying inn-keeper and coachman
and walking through the night into the city, do we catch
a glimpse of the poor lady :

> Behold us then in this expedition ; myself wrapped up in
> a very heavy greatcoat, and my cane in my hand. I did not
> imagine I could have walked a couple of miles in this equipage,
> had my life been depending ; my wife a delicate creature, who

had scarce ever walked a mile in her life ; and the ragamuffin before us with our boxes under his arm. The night was dark and wet ; the road slippery and dirty ; not a soul was seen, nor a sound was heard : all was silent, dreary, and horrible. I laid my account with a violent fit of illness from the cold I should infallibly catch, if I escaped assassination, the fears of which were the more troublesome as I had no weapon to defend our lives. While I laboured under the weight of my greatcoat which made the streams of sweat flow down my face and shoulders, I was plunging in the mud, up to the mid-leg at every step, and at the same time obliged to support my wife, who wept in silence, half dead with terror and fatigue.

Recollecting all these unequal struggles with rapacious inn-keepers and cheating postilions as he wrote in the tranquillity of Nice, Smollett is obliged at last to admit that they were not worth the few sixpences he saved.

The *Travels* is a fine book, worthy to stand beside Fielding's *Voyage to Lisbon* (1754), Sterne's *Sentimental Journey* (1768) and Johnson's *Journey to the Hebrides* (1775). Sterne met Smollett in Rome and in Turin and each time found him fulminating. He caricatured him as Smelfungus in the *Sentimental Journey* and lays his finger on Smollett's weakness for being miserable and angry. ' "I'll tell it", cried Smelfungus, " to the world." " You had better tell it ", I said, "to your physician." ' Good common sense, and Smollett recognized it in the last letters, when he was a much fitter man. He was moving pleasantly towards the self-portrait in *Humphry Clinker*, ' good humoured and civilized '.

There was something in Smollett's nature that irritated him excessively when he saw the cruelty and craft of man to man. Examples occur again and again in the early novels like raw gashes in the comic body of his work. They are more controlled in the *Travels* because his greater power permitted restraint. In his last novel, the masterpiece, they are woven into the comic structure, becoming part of the caricature figures. *Humphry Clinker* is composed with the serenity of mastery. Smollett had at last come to terms with life and expressed his views through the medium of a style that adorns a century of great prose stylists.

Humphry Clinker was published in June 1771, three months before his death. Once again he uses the letter form, and once again, as always, his characters travel. Once again he innovates, for the letters are not written by one character but five, a device only used once before and in verse, in Anstey's *New Bath Guide* (1766). The joy of this method is that episodes are seen through different eyes and the characters comment on one another as their story proceeds.

The chief character and the chief letter writer is Matthew Bramble, who is very largely an ideal self-portrait of Smollett. He is Smollett's vehicle for comment on life, he is the kindly agent for good, exerting to that end his wealth, his experience, and his position. His nephew, Jeremy Melford, writes the other long letters, and these carry the main burden of the story. The other three writers are ladies, as the great novel readers were the ladies and Smollett made few business errors.[1]

Miss Tabitha Bramble was Matthew's sister, a sourly ageing spinster in search of a husband. Lydia Melford was the heroine, and a very pleasant one. Win Jenkins was the comic maid whose letters, happily brief, enjoy like her mistress's the old comedy confusion of misspellings and malapropisms.

For the three ladies there are three men, Lieutenant Lismahago, one of the great English comic characters, Mr. Wilson, and Humphry Clinker himself. Lismahago makes a true comedy entrance :

> A tall, meagre figure, answering, with his horse, the description of Don Quixote mounted on Rozinante, appeared in the

---

[1] 'Tim had made shift to live many years by writing novels, at the rate of five pounds a volume ; but that branch of business is now engrossed by female authors, who publish merely for the propagation of virtue, with so much ease and spirit, and delicacy, and knowledge of the human heart, and all in the serene tranquillity of high life, that the reader is not only enchanted by their genius, but reformed by their morality.'— (*Humphry Clinker*).

twilight at the inn door, while my aunt and Liddy stood at a window in the dining-room. He wore a coat, the cloth of which had once been scarlet, trimmed with Brandenburgs, now totally deprived of their metal; and he had holster-caps and housing of the same stuff and same antiquity. Perceiving ladies at the window above, he endeavoured to dismount with the most graceful air he could assume; but the ostler neglecting to hold the stirrup when he wheeled off his right foot, and stood with his whole weight on the other, the girth unfortunately gave way, the saddle turned, down came the cavalier to the ground, and his hat and periwig falling off, displayed a head-piece of various colours, patched and plastered in a woeful condition. . . .

He would have measured above six feet in height had he stood upright; but he stooped very much; was very narrow in the shoulders, and very thick in the calves of his legs, which were cased in black spatterdashes. As for his thighs, they were long and slender, like those of a grasshopper; his face was at least half a yard in length, brown and shrivelled, with projecting cheek-bones, little grey eyes on the greenish hue, a large hook-nose, a pointed chin, a mouth from ear to ear, very ill furnished with teeth, and a high, narrow forehead, well furrowed with wrinkles. His horse was exactly in the style of its rider; a resurrection of dry bones which (as we afterwards learned) he valued exceedingly, as the only present he had ever received in his life.

Each of the five writers has a brief letter at the beginning which swiftly gives their character, so that in a very few pages all the characters are outlined firmly and a love story is indicated which will no doubt end happily but could hardly be in a more unfortunate state than when the story opens.

The action is mainly in Bath, London, Edinburgh, the Scottish Highlands, and on the Welsh border, and on all the roads between these places. The story stands completely still (it is simple enough and waits easily) during the Scottish tour. It is generally agreed that Smollett wrote a good part of the book during his last stay in Britain, for many of the descriptions of places and of society have the air of recent observation. Matthew Bramble's letter from Bath on 23 April has comments on town planning and architecture

which were surely written on the spot ; and much of the
Scottish tour bears the marks of recent observation. The
final shape, colour, and atmosphere were probably applied
in Italy.

He still does without a plot of any consequence, and relies
instead upon letting his characters travel and meet odd
people and run into odd incidents on the road. The
difference is that he is no longer writing picaresque. He is
celebrating the England and the Scotland in which he has
spent his life. He writes with an exile's love of his native
land and people and this changes and deepens the quality
of his writing. *Humphry Clinker* is one of the great pictures
of eighteenth-century England, a picture of England at a
great moment in her history, a record of a society which
was launching out to change the appearance of half the
world.

It stands with *Tom Jones* and *Tristram Shandy*, *The Decline
and Fall* and the *Speeches On Conciliation*, *The Lives of the
Poets* and *The Vicar of Wakefield* ; and the reader who has
enjoyed them will enjoy *Humphry Clinker* the better. For
these great pieces are nearly two hundred years away now
and though the English character has not changed much and
not advanced on the ideals held then, English society has
changed a great deal. They were written before the Indus-
trial Revolution, the longest and most vile of those com-
paratively bloodless Revolutions that threaten the English
spirit. The spirit of that former age can be recaptured
only by considerable reading of what was thought and
well expressed.

In an extraordinary passage towards the end of *Humphry
Clinker*, Smollett draws a picture of the ideal eighteenth-
century society, which like *The Deserted Village* and other
pieces, records what might have been as if in foreknowledge
of the dark revolution that was on the way. Matthew
Bramble, in his letters about Dennison and Baynard,
expresses the eighteenth-century nostalgia for the ideal
country life, the craving for a well-ordered society based on

the perennial round of toil on the good earth. Our eighteenth century never failed to have a strong feeling of the need for good society in living the good life and Smollett is at pains to show that the good and socially desirable life can be lived in the country. Your town author, then as now, has no doubts on the matter.

There is no warmer passage in the book than the letter from Matthew Bramble, to his friend Baynard, recommending the ideal life of the country gentleman. So the Scots' exile in Italy, who had nearly killed himself in his overworked life in London, comes at the end to subscribe to the country ideals of eighteenth-century England.

Smollett was one of the four writers who set the English novel on its way and his greatness is to be measured partly by the extent to which he inspired later novelists. Hawser Trunnion and his garrison inspired Sterne's Uncle Toby and Corporal Trim. Scott and Dickens acknowledge their debt. There are many others ; and in general it may be claimed that all the novels about the sea and the English sailor descend from him.

The student's assessment must be that Smollett stands high among the four. The ordinary reader to-day may take a different view. If Fielding and Sterne were altogether abstracted from the furniture of our minds, the loss would be more noticeable than if Smollett were taken away. Yet the loss would be great enough if Morgan and Martin Ratlin and Commodore Trunnion were missing ; and the loss of Matthew Bramble and Lieutenant Lismahago would be greater still.

In assessing Smollett we think in terms of the characters he created, so we look back for comparisons over just two centuries of character drawing in the novel. It is a large gallery, with many styles. The reader of George Eliot's *Middlemarch* catches the surprise of style difference when suddenly, during the rich enjoyment of the character play in that novel, someone mentions Smollett. George Eliot uses the rich potentiality of the novel for showing the principal characters developing and modifying by their contact with their environment and more fixed, older characters. The novel moves with the pace of life itself ; the slow years and the sudden crises. At the moment of one of these crises in the life of Dorothea, the heroine, that stupid and sympathetic character, Mr. Brooke, recommends the reading of Smollett to her sick, pedantic husband :

> . . , get Dorothea to read you light things, Smollett, *Roderick Random, Humphry Clinker* : they are a little broad, but she may read anything now she's married, you know. I remember they made me laugh uncommonly—there's a droll bit about a postilion's breeches. We have no such humour now.

Indeed they hadn't. That simple, early novel sort of humour after the quiet, pointed wit of George Eliot is like the guffawing of boys at play. There was an equal difference in the character drawing. Smollett never develops characters. He creates them brilliantly, as we have seen, in a few sentences, then sets them moving and talking among the other characters. He makes them and he is responsible for bringing them together so that the maximum amount of fun is extracted from them. They are comedy characters, created and used in Ben Jonson's way, by interplay without development.

In the guise of Matthew Bramble, Smollett carries his responsibility one stage further. Matthew Bramble concerns himself to help other people and the novel becomes a much more serious consideration of life than his earlier ones. It faces the simple and recurring human problem of living with other people and living one's own life at the same time. Therefore we still turn to Smollett, as we turn to Fielding and Sterne, for that humorous comment on life which is one of the great legacies from our indispensable eighteenth century.

We may regard Smollett as a good European. His novels derive from Cervantes and Le Sage whose works he translated. When he set his factory to translate Voltaire he added the notes on the prose works himself. More generally, like so many of his English contemporaries, he derives from the literature of Rome. His comedy is like Latin comedy. His ideals—of gravity, of humanity, of disciplined industry and the proper organization of all human affairs—are Roman ideals. And his final belief, that man is at his best and happiest in a country society, reminds us of Cicero's words on the farmer's life : ' nothing better, nothing more attractive, nothing more suitable for a free man '.

TOBIAS SMOLLETT
A
Select Bibliography

(Place of publication London, unless stated otherwise.)

Bibliographies :

THE LIFE OF T. G. SMOLLETT, by D. Hannay (1887).
Contains a bibliography by J. P. Anderson.

A STUDY IN SMOLLETT, by H. S. Buck. New Haven (1925).
Contains a complete collation of the first and second editions
of *Peregrine Pickle.*

SMOLLETT ET LA FRANCE, by E. Joliat. Paris (1935).
Contains a bibliography of translations of Smollett's works.

SMOLLETT STUDIES, by C. E. Jones. Los Angeles (1942).
Contains a bibliography.

SMOLLETT'S REPUTATION AS A NOVELIST, by F. W. Boege. Princeton
(1947).
Contains a bibliography.

LETTERS, edited by F. Cordaseo. Madrid (1949).
Contains a bibliography of Collected Editions.

Collected Editions :

PLAYS AND POEMS, with Memoirs of the Life and Writings of the
Author (1777).

MISCELLANEOUS WORKS, containing Novels, Poems, Plays, and
Travels. 6 vols. Edinburgh (1790).

MISCELLANEOUS WORKS, with Memoirs of his Life and Writings
by R. Anderson. 6 vols. Edinburgh (1796).
Reprinted, with enlarged Memoir, 1800.

WORKS, with Memoirs of his Life by J. Moore. 8 vols. (1797).
Reprinted, edited by J. P. Browne, 1872.

NOVELS, with a Memoir by Sir Walter Scott. 2 vols. (1821).
Ballantyne's Novelist's Library, Vols. II and III.

MISCELLANEOUS WORKS, with a Life of the Author. 12 vols.
(1824).

MISCELLANEOUS WORKS, with a Memoir of the Author by T. Roscoe. (1841.)
Frequently reprinted throughout the nineteenth century.

WORKS, selected and edited by D. Herbert, Edinburgh (1870).
Frequently reprinted before the end of the nineteenth century.

WORKS, edited by G. Saintsbury. 12 vols. (1895).
Reprinted 1899, 1902, etc., and by the Navarre Society, 1925.

WORKS edited by W. E. Henley and T. Seccombe. 12 vols. (1899–1901).

WORKS, edited by G. H. Maynardier. 12 vols. New York (1902).

NOVELS. Shakespeare Head Edition. 11 vols. Oxford (1925–6).

Separate Works :

ADVICE : A SATIRE (1746). *Verse.*

REPROOF : A SATIRE (1747). *Verse.*
Reprinted with *Advice,* 1748.

THE ADVENTURES OF RODERICK RANDOM. 2 vols. (1748). *Novel.*

THE REGICIDE : OR, JAMES THE FIRST OF SCOTLAND, A Tragedy. (1749). *Drama.*

THE ADVENTURES OF PEREGRINE PICKLE. 4 vols. (1751). *Novel.*
Revised by the author, 1758.

A FAITHFUL NARRATIVE OF THE BASE AND INHUMAN ARTS THAT WERE LATELY PRACTISED UPON THE BRAIN OF HABBAKKUK HILDING, by Drawcansir Alexander (Tobias Smollett). (1752). *Essay.*

AN ESSAY ON THE EXTERNAL USE OF WATER, WITH PARTICULAR REMARKS UPON THE MINERAL WATERS AT BATH. (1752). *Essay.*
Edited by C. E. Jones, Baltimore, 1935.

THE ADVENTURES OF FERDINAND COUNT FATHAM. 2 vols. (1753). *Novel.*

A COMPENDIUM OF AUTHENTIC AND ENTERTAINING VOYAGES (ed. by T. Smollett). 7 vols. (1756). *Anthology.*

THE REPRISAL : OR, THE TARS OF OLD ENGLAND, a Comedy (1757). *Drama.*

A COMPLETE HISTORY OF ENGLAND FROM THE DESCENT OF JULIUS CAESAR TO THE TREATY OF AIX LA CHAPELLE. 4 vols. (1757–8). *History.*
Second edition, 11 vols., 1758–60.

THE ADVENTURES OF SIR LAUNCELOT GREAVES. 2 vols. (1762). *Novel.*
First published in *The British Magazine*, I, II, 1760–1.

A CONTINUATION OF THE COMPLETE HISTORY, 4 vols. (1760–1). *History.*
A fifth volume was added in 1765. *v.* L. M. Knapp : ' The Publication of Smollett's Complete History and Continuation ' in *The Library* XVI, 1935.

THE PRESENT STATE OF ALL NATIONS (ed. by Smollett). 8 vols. (1768–9). *Anthology.*

TRAVELS THROUGH FRANCE AND ITALY. 2 vols. (1766). *Travel.* Reprinted with Smollett's corrections in ' The World's Classics ', ed. T. Seccombe, 1907.
The Chiltern Library edition (1949) has an introduction by Sir Osbert Sitwell.

THE HISTORY AND ADVENTURES OF AN ATOM. 2 vols. (1769). *Satire.*
Some copies are dated 1749.

THE EXPEDITION OF HUMPHRY CLINKER. 3 vols. (1771). *Novel.*
Vol. I of the first edition is misdated 1671.

ODE TO INDEPENDENCE. Glasgow (1773). *Verse.*

LETTERS HITHERTO UNPUBLISHED. Dumbarton (1859).
See J. Irving's *Some Account of the Family of Smollett of Bonhill* under Critical section.

LETTERS 1721–1771 (1926).
See *The Life and Letters of Tobias Smollett, 1721–1771,* by Lewis Melville, under Critical section.

LETTERS, collected and edited by E. S. Noyes. Cambridge, Mass. (1926).

LETTERS, edited by F. Cordaseo. Madrid (1949).
Contains thirty-one letters unrecorded by Noyes.

Periodicals Edited by Smollett :

THE CRITICAL REVIEW : OR ANNALS OF LITERATURE (1756–90).
Smollett was editor-in-chief from 1756 to 1763, and an occasional contributor thereafter.

THE BRITISH MAGAZINE : OR MONTHLY REPOSITORY (1760–7).

THE BRITON (1762–3).

Smollett also contributed to THE MONTHLY REVIEW. *v.* B. C. Nangle, *The Monthly Review, Indexes of Contributors and Articles,* Oxford (1934).

Translations by Smollett :

THE ADVENTURES OF GIL BLAS, by A. R. Le Sage. 4 vols. (1749).

DON QUIXOTE, by M. de Cervantes Saavedra. 2 vols. (1755).

THE WORKS OF VOLTAIRE (by Smollett and others). 36 vols. (1761–9).
Three volumes were added later. Smollett had only a small part in the translation, but wrote all the historical and critical notes for the volumes completed by May 1763.

THE ADVENTURES OF TELEMACHUS, by F. de Salignac de la Mothe Fénelon. 2 vols. (1776).

Some Critical and Biographical Studies :

LIFE WITH CRITICAL OBSERVATIONS ON HIS WORKS, by R. Anderson. Edinburgh (1820).
In Volume I of Smollett's *Miscellaneous Works,* 6 vols. The best of many memoirs by R. Anderson.

LECTURES ON THE ENGLISH COMIC WRITERS, by W. Hazlitt (1819).

LIVES OF THE NOVELISTS, by Sir Walter Scott (1821).

SOME ACCOUNT OF THE FAMILY OF SMOLLETT OF BONHILL : with a Series of Letters by T. Smollett hitherto unpublished, by J. Irving. Dumbarton (1859).
Reprinted in *The Book of Dumbartonshire* by J. Irving, 3 vols. 1879.

LIFE, by D. Hannay (1887).
In the ' Great Writers Series '. Contains a bibliography by J. P. Anderson.

TOBIAS SMOLLETT, by W. H. O. Smeaton. Edinburgh (1897).
In the ' Famous Scots Series '.

A STUDY IN SMOLLETT, CHIEFLY ' PEREGRINE PICKLE', by H. S. Buck. New Haven (1925).
Includes a scrutiny of the edition of 1758.

TOBIAS SMOLLETT. A STUDY OF HIS MISCELLANEOUS WORKS, by A. Whitridge (1925).

LIFE AND LETTERS 1721–1771, by Lewis Melville (1926).
Lewis Melville is the pseudonym of L. S. Benjamin.

SMOLLETT AS POET, by H. S. Buck. New Haven (1927).

SMOLLETT ET LA FRANCE, by E. Joliat. Paris (1935).
Contains a bibliography of translations of Smollett's works.

THE LATER CAREER OF TOBIAS SMOLLETT, by L. L. Martz. New Haven (1942).

SMOLLETT STUDIES, by C. E. Jones. Los Angeles (1942).
Contains a bibliography.

TOBIAS SMOLLETT. TRAVELER-NOVELIST, by G. M. Kahrl. Chicago (1945).

SMOLLETT'S REPUTATION AS A NOVELIST, by F. W. Boege. Princeton (1947).
Contains a bibliography.

TOBIAS SMOLLETT, DOCTOR OF MEN AND MANNERS, by L. M. Knapp. Princeton (1949).
The fullest modern study.

BRITISH BOOK NEWS

A monthly bibliographical journal designed to acquaint the reader with the best British books on all subjects, including those published in the Commonwealth and Empire. It contains bibliographies of specific subjects and articles of general interest to the bookman. Its most important feature is the Book List, compiled by a number of specialists, which occupies the major part of each issue and provides a critical selection of the most important new books and reprints of all kinds, annotated, classified, and indexed.

1s. per copy (Overseas)

Annual subscription 10s. (Overseas)

Bound volumes, fully indexed, are available as follows through LONGMANS, GREEN & CO., 6 & 7 Clifford Street, London, W.1 : for 1943 and 1944, 6s. net each ; for 1945, 7s. 6d. net ; for 1946, 12s. 6d. net ; for 1947, 15s. net ; for 1948, probably 15s. net.

★

Published for

THE BRITISH COUNCIL

by the National Book League

Address : BRITISH BOOK NEWS, 3 Hanover Street

London, W.1

Supplements to

BRITISH BOOK NEWS

*

Published or in preparation

BERNARD SHAW	A. C. Ward
JOSEPH CONRAD	Oliver Warner
G. K. CHESTERTON	Christopher Hollis
THE BRONTË SISTERS	Phyllis Bentley
HENRY JAMES	Michael Swan
JOHN KEATS	Edmund Blunden
E. M. FORSTER	Rex Warner
T. S. ELIOT	M. C. Bradbrook
ARNOLD BENNETT	Frank Swinnerton
BYRON	Herbert Read
WILLIAM BLAKE	Kathleen Raine
BERTRAND RUSSELL	Alan Dorward
GEORGE ELIOT	Lettice Cooper
OSBERT SITWELL	Roger Fulford
JANE AUSTEN	Sylvia Townsend Warner

Each with a frontispiece ; an introductory essay ;
and a select bibliography

PUBLISHED FOR

THE BRITISH COUNCIL
and the NATIONAL BOOK LEAGUE
by LONGMANS, GREEN & CO.
LONDON. NEW YORK. TORONTO.

1/6 net